Toby Wood

Keep away from children

Toby Wood
23/9/93

cover illustration and drawings
by
Colin Watson

Poetry Now

copyright 1993 Toby Wood

ISBN 1 85731 385 2

Published by
Poetry Now,
1-2 Wainman Road,
Woodston,
Peterborough,
PE2 7BU

Printed in England by
Forward Press. (0733) 230759

Keep away from children

A Special Thank You to

Abbotsmede Junior School, Peterborough
past, future
and currently

Dianne*** Shabeela***Stacey***Kevin***Paul*** Luke***Gavin***Danielle*** Christopher***Sageer***Tanya***Joanne*** Kirsty*** Shaid*** Katy***Ashley***Charlotte***Ian***Mackala***Assia*** Trevor***Julie***Rhona***Azmina***Katie***Hayley***Tina*** Emma***Scarlett***Terrison*** Nicholas***Kerryann*** Sarah***Kaley*** Paul*** John*** Parminder***Darren*****Colin*****Rabin***Stacey*** James***Danielle*** Ryan***Ashley*** Christopher*** Smera*** Claire***Nabeela***Craig*** Zeben***Saima***Elizabeth***Luke***Rebecca***Tina***David***Melissa*** Barry***Adrian***Lee***Ambrose***Daniel*** Sarah***David*** Sherry***Jonathan***Hayley***Robert***Stacey***Louise***Ayshia***Andrew***Nazleen*** Rachel*** Troy*****Jane*****Craig***Brian***Emma***Imran***Luke***Lee***Michelle***Maria***Lee***Karl***Terri***Joleen***Dennis***Donna***Paul*** Steven***Rebecca*** Jason***David*** Sameer***Michael*** Claire***Jaskarn*** Donna*** Brett***Peter*****Kitty*****Waseem***Melissa***Kelly***Charlene***Billy***Michael***Azher***Ashley***Emma***Atif***Rehana***Paul***Martin***Clive***Christopher***Nicholas***Richard***Tasnime***Paula***Paul***Donna***Amy***Sajjaad***Daniel***Amanda***Lyndsay*****Meg*****Aaron*** Bushra*** Louise***Stephen***Saalma***Richard***Munir***Duane***Colin***Ashley***Kirsty***John***Gareth***Matthew***Sarah***Richard***Michael***Shabir***Phillip***John***Charlene***Simon***Shahzad***Michael*** Zoe*****Jean***** Lindsey***Sue***Bridget***Roy***Stacia***Farat***Sue***Huw***June***Sylvia***Barbara***Lynette***Penny***Linda***Marion*** Zebun***Sheila***Sue***Margaret***Shirley***John***Jan***Judy***Gerry*** Joan***Helga***Dave***Tracy***Viv***Bev***Jane***Elaine***Pauline***Marion and the infs***Oliver

and, of course,

Irene, Rebecca and Daniel

contents

the first poem in the book	1
I'm lucky	2
My Little Brother	4
Sister Sarah	6
mysteries	8
Leaving the favourite bit 'til last	10
My Legs Ache	12
Underneath the Bedclothes	14
Fresh Air, Peace and Quiet	18
The Most Dangerous Place....	20
Disaster	24
Recipe for Dragon Steaks	27

All I want is...	28
Teachers are like dragons	31
Alphabet Register	32
Song of the Balding Teacher	33
The Speck of Dust	34
Have any of you seen my stapler?	37
painting	38
Tony Benton's Sandwiches	40
Bringing pets to school	43
Swimming Lesson	46
Handstands	48
Cliff Richard	50

the first poem in the book

the first poem in the book
is not
the biggest or the smallest
the shortest or the tallest
the thinnest or the fattest
the oldest or the youngest
the wisest or the daftest
the dullest or the brightest
but I can promise this to you
it certainly is the firstest

I'm Lucky...

I'm lucky...
I've got...

    all I need to live
 a **b**ike to get me around
    clothes to keep me warm
    domestic appliances like a cooker,
                      fridge or iron
    electricity that I can switch off and on
    family and friends
 a **g**arden with grass and flowers
 a **h**ouse to live in made of bricks
    imagination so that I can pretend or
                    make believe
a **j**ob that earns me money
    knowledge - things that I can learn or
                    find out about
    limbs - hands to write and to hold,
        legs to walk and to run

    plenty to eat
    questions to ask and a brain to help me
                      answer them
a **r**adio to tell me what's happening
   sight - to see all around and beyond
a **t**elly that I can watch and watch and watch
    United - Peterborough United, the best
      football team in the world (well nearly!)
   vocal chords so that I can talk to anyone
                      I want
  water to drink and to wash in
 exercise to keep me fit and healthy
  you - to be here with me
  Zzzz. ..I can't think of anything for 'z'

  Can you?

My little Brother

My little brother
is three years younger than me.
So when I was eight he was five.
We used to share bunks
in the same bedroom.
Because I was older I was on top
and he was on the bottom.
When Mum put the light out and we were
in the dark alone
I used to make strange noises
to frighten him.
Whooo...whooo...
He would cry, "Mum...Mum!"
Mum used to come back up the stairs.
She would say,
   "Now stop that, you're frightening him."
When she had gone back down the stairs
I would say to him,
   "Trying to get me into trouble, eh!
   You wait - I'll get you for that."

So when he was nearly asleep
I would raise my mattress just a little bit
so that I could see him underneath.
I would get bits of fluff or tiny bits of paper,
roll them up in my fingers and
flick them down onto his face.
His nose would twitch and
his head would quiver.
After a while he would cry...
"Mum, Mum, I'm scared...
something's hitting my face."
Mum would come back up the stairs.
   "Don't worry, dear," she'd say,
   "get back to sleep."
I would lie there
motionless
like a log
just grinning to myself.
Mum would go back downstairs again.
   "There you are," I'd whisper, "Got you."
It must have been horrible being
my little brother.

Sister Sarah

My sister Sarah is six years younger than me.
She always has been.
When she was born I was six;
when she was ten I was sixteen
and when I wrote this she was thirty two
and I was......
well work it out for yourself!

I remember when she was born.
She was born at home.
I heard this cry from upstairs
and my dad came down and said,
"You've got a little sister."
"Wow," I thought,
"Big Deal."

I was expected to look after her,
be nice to her, be kind to her.
She got away with **MURDER**.
She never got told off when her bedroom was untidy.
I did.
She never got told off when she broke something.
I did.
She never got told off when she was naughty.
I did.

She had tight dark brown curly hair
that covered her head like a
thorny halo.
She looked so sweet.
Sweet!
If only you knew her.
Now she's got even longer tight curly dark brown
hair,
long dangly earrings,
bright red lips
and she talks all the time.
She always was good at talking.
My sister holds the World Record for Talking.
She started when she was one month old
and is still going strong
all these years later.
She's talked for all that time
without taking a breath.
Nobody can get a word in
edgeways, longways, Sideways or crossways.
She's got a job taking tourists round London.
She talks to them all the time.
Incredible, isn't it?
Being paid all that money
for doing the one thing she's good at;
talking.

mysteries

for years and years and years
every time I saw a cauliflower
I could never understand
why the middle bit was creamy white
and the outside pieces green

for years and years and years
every time I smelled an onion
I could never understand
why it made me cry

for years and years and years
every time I felt a strawberry
I could never understand
why it had little hairs on it

for years and years and years
every time I saw a banana
I could never understand
why it was curved

for years and years and years
every time I looked at pieces of cheese
I could never understand
why they were different shades of
white, yellow and orange

for years and years and years
every time I bought an ice lolly
I could never understand
how they got the stick in the middle

for years and years and years
every time I ate a curry
I could never understand
why it made me hot and bothered

for years and years and years
I wondered all these things
I know the answers to some of them
but not all
Some of them remain
to this day
mysteries

Leaving the favourite bit 'til last

When I was young
and at home
with my mum, my dad, my brother and sister
we ate our meals all together.
Mum would put a plate of food in front of me.
I would look at it very carefully
and then make a
VERY IMPORTANT DECISION.
Which bit was I going to save 'til last?

Sometimes it would be the potato and gravy,
sometimes the baked beans
or the toast underneath.
I would start eating
and my dad would say,
"I hope you're going to eat all that up.
You're not going to waste any, are you?"
"No, dad," I would say,
"I'm just leaving the favourite bit 'til last."
My dad would smile.
I could tell that he used to do just the same
when he was a boy.

Today,
when my own family sits down to a meal,
my son looks at his plate.
I can tell that he's making a
VERY IMPORTANT DECISION.
"I hope you're going to eat all that up," I say.
"Yes, dad," he says,
"I'm just leaving the favourite bit 'til last."

Some things never change.

My Legs Ache

Dad, my legs ache
I'm fed up
Fed up of walking all this way

Not long now, we're going home soon

Dad, my feet hurt
My shoe's rubbing
And my laces keep coming undone

Never mind - try to forget about it

Dad, I've got something in my eye
And it hurts
And it's making me cry

Don't rub it then - it'll only make it worse

Dad, I want to go to the toilet
I can't wait any longer
I think I'm going to burst

I told you to go before we came out

Dad, how much longer before we go home?
I've got what I want
And I'm bored

Not long now - we've nearly finished

Dad, my legs ache
I'm fed up
Fed up of walking all this way

Well why don't you get back in your pushchair then?

NO - I'M A BIG BOY NOW!

UNDERNEATH the Bedclothes

I'd had my bath,
brushed my teeth,
and 'sorted myself out'
(as my Mum is always telling me to do).
Then it was time to go to bed.
Mum gave me a kiss 'Good Night';
you know the sort,
a big mushy kiss.
SLURRRRP!!!

Her footsteps gradually faded
as she went downstairs to watch the telly.
I was alone.
"Now," I thought,
"I'm not tired yet;
What shall I do?
I know - I'll have an ADVENTURE
underneath the bedclothes."

I got ready for the Great Expedition.
I got my school bag with my P. E. kit
in case I needed a change of clothes.
I got my Teddy Edward,
my trusty companion
and sharer of many previous adventures.

I got my colouring book
and a couple of felt tip pens
just in case I got bored.
And off I went.

Shuffle, shuffle, shuffle;
Grope, grope, grope;
Jiggle, jiggle, jiggle.

Down and down I went,
deeper and deeper,
until the light at the top of the bed
got further and further away.
Soon there was no light at all, just pitch black.

I was all on my own - alone;
thousands of miles away from civilisation,
in a place where no-one had been before.

I looked around;
saw nothing.
Of course I didn't!
Everything was pitch black, remember!

Then I heard a noise!
A strange noise.
First of all a clumping sound;
Clump, clump, clump...
Then a swishing sound;
Swish, swish, swish...
Then a breathing sound;
Wheew, wheew, wheew...
The hairs on the back of my neck stood on end;
My head slowly sank into my neck;
My bottom lip began to tremble.
I thought I was going to cry.

"*Help!*" I mouthed but no sound came out.
My imagination was racing through my head
as fast as my heart was pounding.
What was it that was getting
closer and closer?

I could just see it now...
a huge slimy green dragon
clump, clump, clumping towards me.
    I could just hear it now...
    a huge slimy green man-eating dragon
    swish, swish, swishing towards me.
        I could just feel it now...
        a huge slimy, green man-eating
        ever-so hungry dragon
        breathing hot, baking, dreadful fire
        right down my neck...

Suddenly my dark bed-clothed world was
shattered.
The sky seemed to move and,
all of a sudden,
there was light again.
And there...
And there stood...
And there stood...
MY DAD
with a great big grin on his face.

"What are you up to?" he said,
"I thought your mum told you to get to sleep.
Come on, you've got school in the morning.
Stop playing about and get some sleep.
You'll be too tired to do any work and then what
will your teacher say?"

"Yes Dad, good night Dad," I muttered.
He tucked me up nice and warm.
I turned over and closed my eyes.
It was then I remembered
poor old Teddy Edward
down at the bottom of the bed.
Oh well, I'd better rescue him tomorrow night.

Fresh Air, Peace and Quiet

Ahhh.....
Fresh Air, Peace and Quiet.
Standing on a hillside
looking around;
Fresh Air, Peace and Quiet.
Strange really...
There's no such thing as
Quiet.
Listen...
You may think that it's quiet but
there are still noises near and far;
listen.

someone coughing
a car door slams
the buzz of a motor bike
the creak of a door
the bark of a dog
the gentle sigh of people breathing
the distant murmur of voices

Is there such a thing as
Fresh Air?
I suppose there is
but there are so many
chemicals, germs and invisible rays
floating around
I begin to wonder.

The Most Dangerous Place....

Yesterday I went on an adventure;
a trip to a place full of
danger and dread.
I came home from school,
back through the winding streets
until, at last, I was there.
I had arrived at the place
where my adventure was going to begin.
I walked up towards the front door,
took a key out of my pocket
and let myself in.
It was dark and cold.
I reached out and flicked a switch.
The light came on.
I went straight into the kitchen
and washed my hands.
They were mucky because I had been playing football.
I fancied a cup of tea
so I walked across to the kettle
and was just about to switch it on
when a little voice said to me,
        "Be careful - never switch on anything
        electrical without making sure
        that your hands are dry."

I went back and dried my hands,
switched the kettle on
and made myself
a cup of tea.
I also had   2 chocolate biscuits
                3 digestives
                4 rich tea biscuits and
                a bag of cheese and onion crisps.

It was then I saw a container with some
powder in it.
Oh, how I wished it was sherbet
or some other sort of sweet.
But I wasn't daft.
I could see that it was a little pile of cleaning powder.
My mum must have left the packet out
and it must have spilt.

Funny how it looks the same as sherbet.
I'd better leave it 'til Mum gets home.

I was really thirsty;
playing football at my school is very thirsty work.
What could I have to drink?
I went to the cupboard, pulled it open
and took out a plastic bottle.

"That's no good," I thought,
"That's bleach!
I'd be a right nutter to touch that."
So I carefully put it back thinking how daft my
mum was to put it in the same cupboard as the orange squash.
I also spotted, in the same cupboard,
a bottle of whisky.
Dad has a drink of that at Christmas.
What a daft place to put it - just next to my orange squash.
Ah, there it is - my orange squash.
Just the job for a thirsty midfielder like me
I made myself a glass.
That's better.

I sat down, still hungry.
I could murder some sweets!
I looked in another cupboard,
took out another bottle.
Cor! They look nice;
pretty little red and blue things like licorice torpedoes.
But wait a minute!
They're the pills that Grandad uses for his bad chest.
Fancy putting them there!
Just where I could pick them up
and gobble them all up.
Daft old Grandad.
What are they trying to do to me;
put me in hospital!
I put them back.
I'm still hungry;
really fancy an apple.
I go to the cutlery drawer and feel for a knife.
Ouch!
That one's sharp!
Daft old Mum!
Fancy keeping the sharpest one of the lot just
where I could get it.

21

She should have learnt by now that I'm
accident prone,
especially on my own.

Blimey!
It's cold in here.
I want to warm myself up.
How can I do that?
Light the oven and turn on the heat?
You must think I'm barmy!
Pick up the matches and set light to the sofa?
They must think I'm stupid,
leaving all these things around the house
for me to find.

Better wait until Mum gets home
so that she can switch the fire on.

It was then that I started to feel **CROSS**.
My Mum, Dad and Grandad must be mad!
Leaving all those dangerous things
around the house
for me to find:
THE POWDER
    THE BLEACH
        THE PILLS
            THE KNIFE
                THE MATCHES

They must think I'm completely off my rocker!
I'm really going to tell them what I think when
they get home.
Leaving all those dangerous things around the
house.
At least I'm not daft;
I'm not simple or confused
but what would have happened if someone
with no common sense
had come home first?
Then our house really would have been
**THE MOST
DANGEROUS PLACE IN THE WORLD.**

There's four in my family,
well five if you count the cat.
There's Irene, my wife,
and Becky who's thirteen
and Daniel who's nine.
At least that's how old they were at the time of
the DISASTER.
We were all sitting down to have tea
round the table.
I can't remember exactly what we had to eat
but I do remember that it was
Something and Chips
because, when we have chips,
we always have
Tomato Sauce.
Becky had just turned the bottle upside-down
and given herself
a Dollop.
She put the bottle back
in the middle of the table with the top back on.
At least that's what I thought.
I could have sworn she'd put the top back on;
I was **SURE** she'd put the top back on;
I was **CERTAIN** she'd put the top back on;
I was **POSITIVE** she'd put the top back on.
I reached across;
I grasped the bottle;
I held it high
and **SHOOK** it.

The top flew off and clattered against the radiator
closely followed by lashings of tomato sauce.
Like a volcano erupting the molten lava
sprayed in all directions.
Irene was the first to suffer.
She was only slightly wounded.
A few flecks splattered on her jumper.
Daniel dived for cover;
he's good at avoiding things.
The sauce sprayed over him
and splattered against the wall,
my newly painted magnolia wall,
like bullets from a machine gun...
Chugga...chugga...chugga...chugga...
The hail of bullets flew around the room.
Becky was not so lucky.
She was just raising her fork to her mouth to
take the first morsel of food when
SPLAT!!!
    ZAP!!!
        KERPOW!!!
            SCHLOCK!!!
American Comic Book Stuff.
She leapt backwards, critically wounded,
screaming hysterically,
Aaaaaaaaaaaaaaaaaaargh!!!
It was like one of those nasty videos;
Curse of the Flying Sauce
Rambo 5
Spiller Killer.
She looked down at the damage.
Her white school blouse covered with
Ugly Red Roses.
"What did you do that for?" she yelled.
"I'm sorry," I muttered,
"I thought the top was on."

My face was wearing a stupid embarrassed grin.
The three of them were glaring at me,
their mass murderer dad.
Nervously I said,
"I'll go and get some kitchen roll."
"It'll take more than kitchen roll," Irene said.
The rest of the meal was finished in
angry silence.

For weeks afterwards
we had flecks of tomato sauce
on the table
on the wall
on the ceiling
on the floor.
I was never allowed to forget it.
So now, when we sit down to a meal,
I always shout a warning

DUCK!

P.S.

Luckily the manufacturers of tomato sauce
found out about the 'Disaster' and now put
tomato sauce in squeezy plastic bottles that
are perfectly safe. That's what they think!

Recipe for Dragon Steaks

Take one steak of dragon
Place in a hot oven - Gas mark 7
And cook for 20 minutes
Or for however long it takes you to get
                                      bored.
Then
Remove the steak,
Place it on a serving dish
And scrape iron filings all over.
Not too many,
Not too few.
Then get four dog hairs
And place them lightly on each side of
the dish.

Next
Take a bottle of washing-up liquid
And squirt generously all over.
This will make the steak light and
frothy.
Then take twenty clippings of toe-nails
And lightly sprinkle on the top.
Lastly,
Just to add a touch of colour,
Stir in a can of paint,
Gloss if possible,
But vinyl matt will do.

Then return the whole dish to the oven
And cook until
Nasty, charred, burnt and hard.

Remove from the oven and serve to
someone you don't like very much.

All I want is...

When I was very tiny,
when I was very small
I spent most of the time
learning to talk and crawl.
When Mum gave me milk
I'd just yell and bawl;
baby food, mashed food;
didn't like it at all.
I gurgled...

>   **You can
>   forget your yoghurt
>   forget your greens
>   all I want is...
>   BAKED BEANS**

Soon came my fifth birthday
and off I went to school;
I wasn't very clever,
in fact I was a fool.
I never learnt nuffink,
Was as stubborn as a mule;
stayed for school dinners;
we had mince as a rule.
I complained...

>   **You can
>   forget your yoghurt
>   forget your greens
>   all I want is...
>   BAKED BEANS**

I remember one Christmas
I had a devilish plan;
down our chimney
came this fat bearded man.
He said,
"What do you want for Christmas,
son,
I'll get it if I can."
I plucked up courage
and up to him I ran.
I shouted...

    You can
    forget your yoghurt
    forget your greens
    all I want is...
    BAKED BEANS

When I became sixteen
I finally left home;
I thought that I would travel far;
Around the world I'd roam;
tried many exotic dishes,
rice, curries, minestrone
but I missed my favourite food;
I told Mum on the phone.
I moaned...

    You can
    forget your yoghurt
    forget your greens
    all I want is...
    BAKED BEANS

I went for a job in teaching;
it sounded rather good
but I didn't last long;
I wasn't in the mood;
Thought I'd be a boxer
but my Mum she disapproved
so I ended up in politics,
the Minister of Food.
I argued...

> **You can
> forget your yoghurt
> forget your greens
> all I want is...
> BAKED BEANS**

And now I am withered,
wrinkled, old and grey;
I just watch telly
and sit around all day.
Meals on Wheels comes;
my dinner's on a tray;
but I lift up the lid
and look in dismay.
I croak...

> **You can
> forget your yoghurt
> forget your greens
> all I want is...
> BAKED BEANS**

Teachers are like dragons

Why?

Because when they tell you off they drag

on and on and on and on and on and on and on
and on and on and on and on and
on and on and on and on and on and on and
on and on and on and on..........

Alphabet Register
(No-one's Here)

Andrew's broken his right arm
Barry isn't here
Clare's been sick all night and
Darren's got an aching ear
Eddie's gone to the dentist
Farah's in Pakistan
Gary's gone to buy new shoes
Hazel's gone out with Ann
Ian's still playing football
John is always skiving
Katie's got a broken leg and
Lesley's just arriving
Mark has gone on holiday and
Noreen's gone to town
Oliver is helping his dad and
Patrick's fallen down
Qadir - don't know where he is
Ruby's banged her head
Sophie's at the doctor's
Tony's still in bed
Ursula has got a very bad cold
Vicky - she's got nits
William is down with the 'flu
AleX's shoe's don't fit
Yvonne's gone to see Granny
Zoe's mum has phoned

There's no-one here to teach today
So I might as well go home

32

Song of The Balding Teacher

This morning...
   Lucy, is that you?
This morning I...
   Lucy, please don't talk
This morning I want...
   Lucy, leave her hair alone
This morning I want to...
   Lucy, there's no need to touch them now
This morning I want to talk...
   Lucy, I've told you once before
This morning I want to talk to...
   Lucy, please don't interfere
This morning I want to talk to you...
   Lucy, I can still hear your voice
This morning I want to talk to you about...
   Lucy, I can see you, you know
This morning I want to talk to you about the...
   Lucy, how many more times?
This morning I want to talk to you about the problems...
   Lucy, I don't want to have to get cross with you
This morning I want to talk to you about the problems of...

  of...

   ..of...

Oh, I've forgotten what I wanted to say.

The Speck of Dust (for Mr Cash)

I've got a teacher
Who likes things
Lovely and Clean;
As clean as a new pin.
At the end of every morning;
At the end of every afternoon;
We tidy up the tables
We tidy up our trays
We tidy up everything.
And then
Only then
If everything is clean and tidy
We can go.
One day he said to us,
"Right, I don't want a speck of dust in
this classroom."
We spent ages
polishing....scrubbing....
scrubbing.... polishing....
Until everything was gleaming bright.
Then we all sat up ready to go.
Lorraine saw it first.
She nudged me and whispered,
"Look, over there - coming in through
the door!"
I looked and there it was;
A speck of dust
Floating down through a shaft of light
from the window.
It wasn't a speck of our dust.
It must have come from next door.

I nudged Billy
And he nudged Jane
She nudged Shahzad
And he nudged Shane.
Soon the whole class was looking
skyward
Towards the evil speck of dust.
If Sir spotted it we were sunk;
He'd never let us out.
The speck of dust was floating
down, down, down
Towards the floor.
I carefully edged my chair backwards
And slowly rose from my seat.
Then, in one swift, cat-like movement,
I dived like a goalkeeper
Right across the room
And scooped it up in my hand,
Holding tight.
The whole class stood up and cheered
As if I had just saved a penalty
In the last minute
Of the FA Cup Final at Wembley.
I mopped my brow,
Walked proudly over to my teacher
And brushed the speck of dust into the
bin.
He smiled
And patted me on the shoulder.
"Well Done, Shilton," he said.
"Right everyone,
You can all go out to play."

Have any of you seen my stapler?

Have any of you seen my stapler?
Can you please look on the floor?
I had it just a minute ago;
I might have left it by the door.

I know I had it earlier;
I know I've used it today;
I remember using it to put up
The dinosaur display.

But now I just can't find it;
This really is a pest
'Cos I know that earlier
It was sitting on my desk.

Oh, thank you Clive, you've found it;
You really are a star;
I knew it was round here somewhere;
It couldn't have gone far.

Have any of you seen my staples?
I had them yesterday;
As soon as we have found them
You can all go out to play.

No, not those ones Tracy;
Those ones will not fit;
Oh, where have I put the wretched things?
I am a silly twit.

Oh, I suppose they'll turn up sometime;
My head is in a spin;
Forget the staples - I'll just use
My box of drawing pins.

paint on my jumper
paint up my nose
my mum will kill me
if she gets to know
paint on my elbow
paint on my face
blue paint, red paint
all over the place
paint on the table
teacher going mad
I knew I should have brought
an old shirt of dad's
paint on the floor
paint in the sink
this painting lark's
harder than you think

too much hurry
too much rush
I use my fingers
the others use a brush
everybody getting on
they're all right
they've got paint on their paper
but mine's still white
all the kids have finished
it's time to go
what shall I call my blank sheet?
I know, I'll call it 'SNOW'

Tony Benton's Sandwiches

It was a cold and dreary
November day;
the sort that's wet
but it's not raining.
I was walking down the corridor
when Tony Benton came up to me
and said,
"I've lost my packed lunch.
I put it in the trolley
but it's
gone
disappeared
vanished."
"Oh", I said, "we'd better have a look.
What's it in?"
"A plastic bag."
"Where did you put it?"
"In the trolley."
"When did you last have it?"
"Just a minute ago."
We searched high and low;
in the corridor
in the cloakroom
in the classroom
everywhere.
No packed lunch.
We went into the playground.
"Anybody seen Tony's sandwiches?"
I shouted.

"Yes", said Lee and Dale,
"he had them a minute ago."
I frowned and raised one eyebrow.
"What do you mean - a minute ago?"
"It's true", they said, "he had them...
just a minute ago."
"Tony... is this true?" I said in my
stern voice.
"No", Tony replied, "they've gone...
somebody's got them."
Then Dale told me,
"Tony was walking along throwing his
sandwiches up in the air;
UP....CATCH
UP....CATCH
UP....GONE!!! On the roof!"
"Tony!" I said,
"Have your sandwiches gone on the roof?"
"No no no no no no."

I had had enough of this.
I was going to solve the mystery
ONCE AND FOR ALL.........
I asked three children to come with me
to fetch
the LADDER.
So off we went to fetch
the LADDER.
Others held the bottom while I climbed up,
swung a leg
and clambered up
onto the roof.

And there they were -
sandwiches in a plastic bag
just sitting there waiting to be rescued.
I picked them up and went back down
the LADDER.
"Tony, COME HERE!!!"I yelled.
"Are these your sandwiches?"
"No, they're not mine......
They're someone else's......
I've never seen them before in my life."
He folded his arms,
lowered his head
and sulked.
"I tell you what," I said,
"You can have these sandwiches
that I found on the roof.
I'm sure that nobody will mind.
No-one's come to me to claim them
so you can have them."
"I won't eat them - they're not mine!!!"
Tony said again.
For the rest of lunchtime he just sat there but,
at the end of lunchtime, when we were all
going back to our own classes Jason came up
to me and confidentially whispered, "They
were his sandwiches. He told me they were.
And he's eaten them now - they've all gone!"

The moral of this story
The message in this tale
Is that I found out the FACTS
Thanks to Lee and Dale.
So next time something happens
And your lunch goes on the roof
Don't waste time in lying
Just try and tell the TRUTH!

Bringing pets to school

Kathryn brought her pet fly to school;
She brings it now and then.
She put it on her table
to show her class and friends.

It was seen by Karl's pet spider
which hadn't yet been fed.
The spider leapt and bit it,
leaving it for dead.

Billy's mouse was watching
and rushed across the floor.
It jumped and ate the spider;
Karl's spider was no more.

Now Martin had brought in his pigeon
that he keeps in a shed near his house.
His pigeon thinks mice are tasty
so you can guess the fate of the mouse.

Rose's rat heard the fuss and commotion
and, although it was feeling tired,
floored the poor bird with a stunning right hook.
Martin's pigeon thus expired.

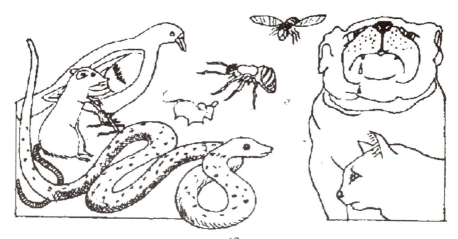

Now not a lot of people know
that Anthony keeps snakes.
He'd brought one in and it loves rats
despite the stomach aches.

The snake lay back quite satisfied
but it was soon outsmarted
by Shabir's usually friendly cat;
the snake is now departed.

The contented cat lay licking its paws
when the rottweiler woke up;
the one brought in by with Jason;
the rottweiler thought, "What luck!"

Now rottweilers love children
for breakfast, dinner and tea
and I'm still hiding behind the door.
Will someone please come and
rescue me!

Swimming Lesson

We're all going swimming
In the Learner Pool;
Going down the steps
The water's rather cool.

Simon's got his armbands;
Lisa's got a float
But I'm so cold
I'm still wearing my coat.

Standing in the corner
Like a block of ice;
My zip's going rusty;
This isn't very nice.

Watch out, here comes the teacher
Telling me to try;
I don't want to do it
So I just stand and cry.

I hate swimming;
I haven't got the strength
So I watch all the others
Doing widths and lengths.

It's been like this once a week
For years and years,
Standing in a corner
Shivering with fear.

It's all right for you youngsters;
You're fearless and bold
But I still can't get the hang of it
Even though I'm forty-two years old!

Thank goodness, the lesson's ended;
I breathe a sigh;
Get out, take my coat off
And rub myself dry.

I wish I wasn't cowardly,
Skinny, scared and weak;
But I'll try and forget about it
Until this time next week!

Handstands

Ellen Jane McKenzie,
a normal little child;
she wasn't daft or silly,
brainless, bad or wild.

She used to play in the playground
at her friendly local school;
she'd play tiggy, sometimes skipping;
safe games as a rule.

Then one day some girls showed her
a new exciting game;
against a wall and upside-down;
handstands is its name.

She thought that she would try it,
this brand new game to play;
she lost her balance, slipped and fell;
head fell off and rolled away.

Her mum and dad were contacted
and looked at their headless daughter with fright
'cos when you've got a headless daughter
you can't kiss her 'Good Night'.

This story didn't really happen;
it simply isn't true.
But I say, "No more handstands, please
or it could happen to you."

(This poem was written instead of a 'telling off' assembly.)

Cliff Richard

Years ago,
when I was quite small,
there was this song by a man called Cliff Richard.
It went, 'We're all going on a Summer Holiday;
    No more working for a week or two.'
And this song came from a film.
Cliff and his mates got on this
red double-decker bus
and drove off to Spain or Greece
(I can't remember which).
They slept on the bus,
   ate on the bus,
   had fun on the bus.
I really liked those bits of the film.
Trouble was Cliff and his mates met these girls.
That's when the film got sloppy and I lost interest.
But, the other day, I got thinking about
that old double-decker bus
and, as I thought, my eyes began to glint and
my mind began to think.

Wouldn't it be great if each of our classes had a
double-decker bus.
Instead of coming to school and going to the
same old classroom,
looking out of the same old window
at the same of rooftops
and the same old sky,
we could have all our lessons on the bus.
We could live on it,
    sleep on it,
        have fun on it.
We could have beds upstairs.
They would have to be bunk beds so that
everyone would fit.
I suppose the upstairs bit would have to have
curtains so that we wouldn't get woken up by the
sun first thing in the morning,
In the downstairs bit we would have
tables and chairs so that we could do our work
and eat our meals.
We would have a little kitchen so that we could
cook all our meals.
We would have to have a sink and water and a
bath or shower, I suppose.
(We'd all get a bit smelly if we didn't wash
sometimes).

We'd have carpets all over.
We'd have a telly and a video so that would mean
we'd need an aerial somewhere on top.

I suppose I'd have to do the driving;
I'm the only one old enough to have one of those
special licences that allows you to drive buses.
Oh, it would be great.

We could drive all over the world;
to Pakistan to visit Qadir's relatives;
Kate could show us round France and Spain
(she's been there before).
I would take you to South America to see the
mountains and the forests.
I've always wanted to go there.
You would all have to bring sensible footwear
because we'd do quite a lot of walking and some
plimsolls or trainers to wear indoors so that we
wouldn't get mud on the carpets.
Oh it would be great!
If we saw something in the news about
flood disasters in Bangladesh
we could go and help.
We wouldn't have to read about foreign places.
We could just go there.
We wouldn't need to do much writing or Maths or
anything like that.
There wouldn't be enough time.
We'd be too busy
going places,
seeing things,
doing things.

Oh, it would be great.
And we'd come back just in time for the
Summer Holidays,
see our mums and dads again,
have a really good wash,
tell gran all about it,
see all our friends again,
get the bus serviced
and then,
in September,
when it was time to go back to school,
we could do it
all
over
again.

go for it!